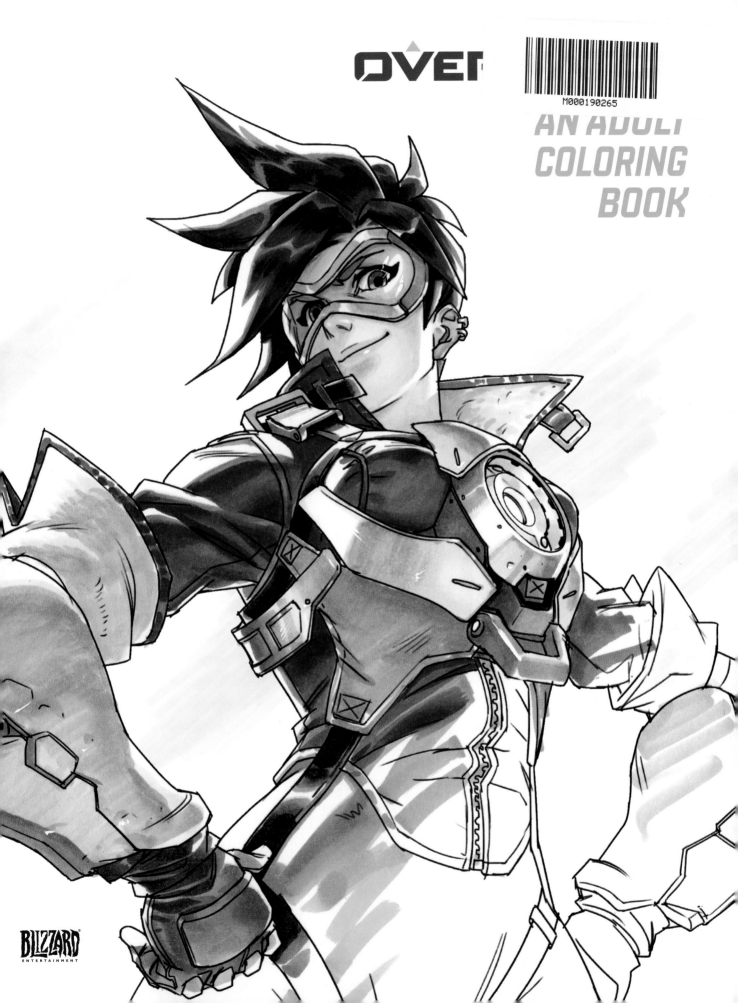

©2017 BLIZZARD ENTERTAINMENT, INC.
ALL RIGHTS RESERVED. OVERWATCH, THE OVERWATCH LOGO, AND BLIZZARD ENTERTAINMENT ARE TRADEMARKS AND/OR REGISTERED TRADEMARKS OF BLIZZARD ENTERTAINMENT, INC. IN THE U.S. AND/OR OTHER COUNTRIES. NO PORTION OF THIS BOOK MAY BE REPRODUCED OR TRANSMITTED IN ANY FORM OR BY ANY MEANS WITHOUT WRITTEN PERMISSION FROM THE COPYRIGHT HOLDERS.

OVERWATCH: AN ADULT COLORING BOOK

CREDITS

TRACER COVER ART
ARNOLD TSANG

D.VA COVER ART
ROMAN KENNEY

EDITORS
ROBERT SIMPSON, CATE GARY, AND ALLISON MONAHAN

ART DIRECTOR
ROMAN KENNEY

ASSISTANT ART DIRECTOR, OVERWATCH
ARNOLD TSANG

LICENSED PRODUCT DEVELOPER
SEAN WANG

PRODUCER
BRIANNE M LOFTIS

SENIOR MANAGER, GLOBAL LICENSING AND PUBLISHING
BYRON PARNELL

DIRECTOR, MANUFACTURING
ANNA WAN

DIRECTOR, CREATIVE DEVELOPMENT
RALPH SANCHEZ

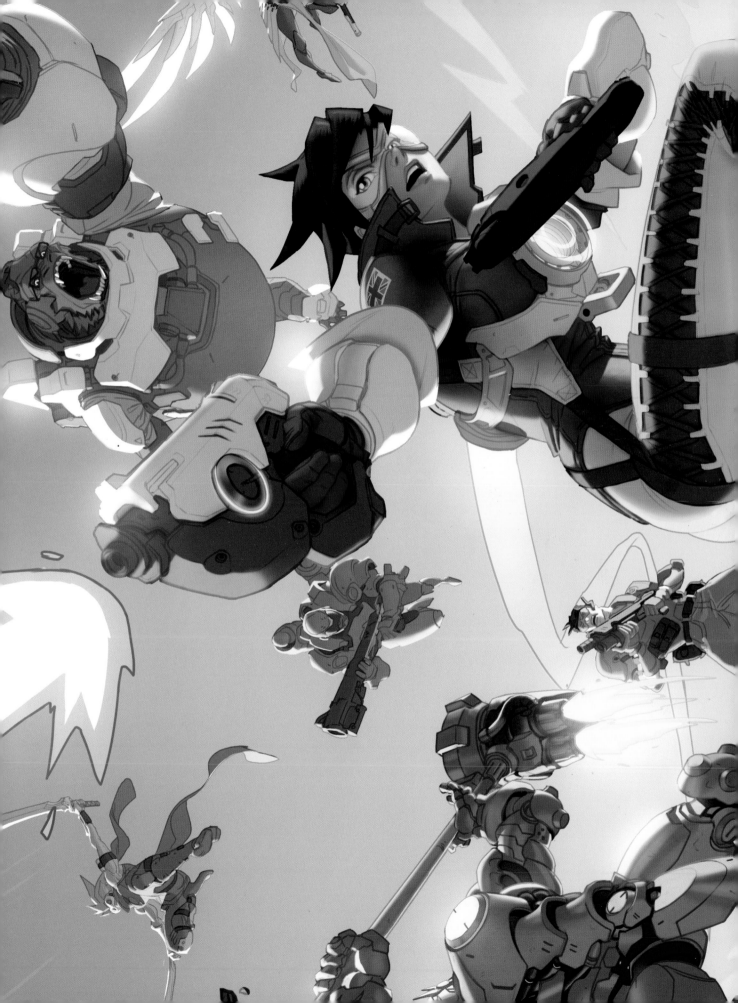

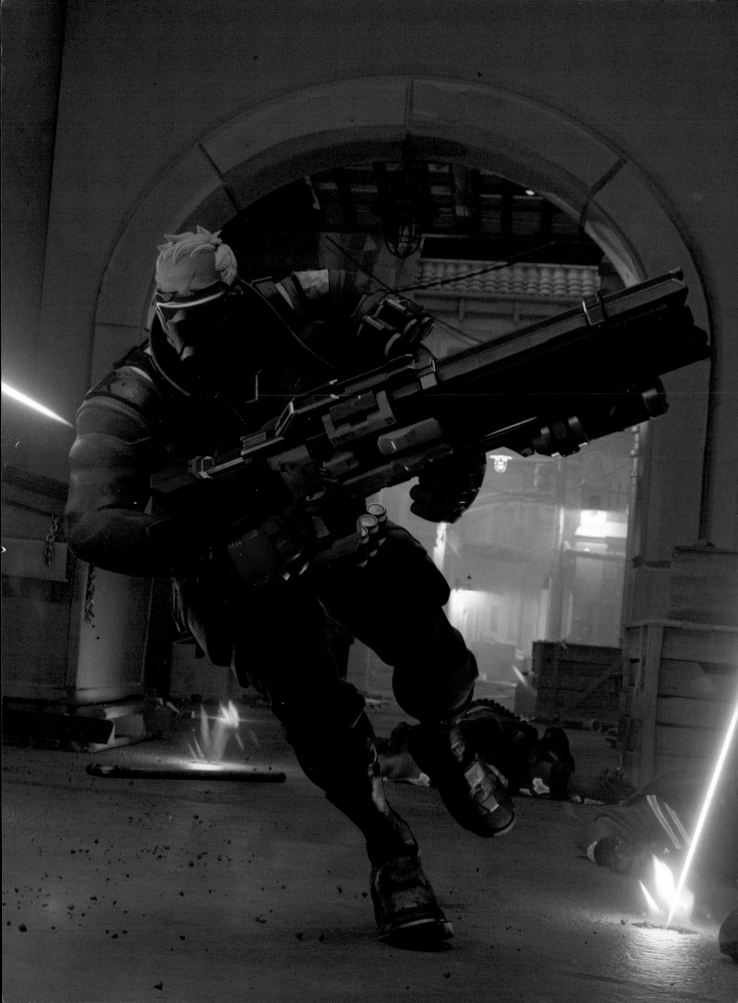

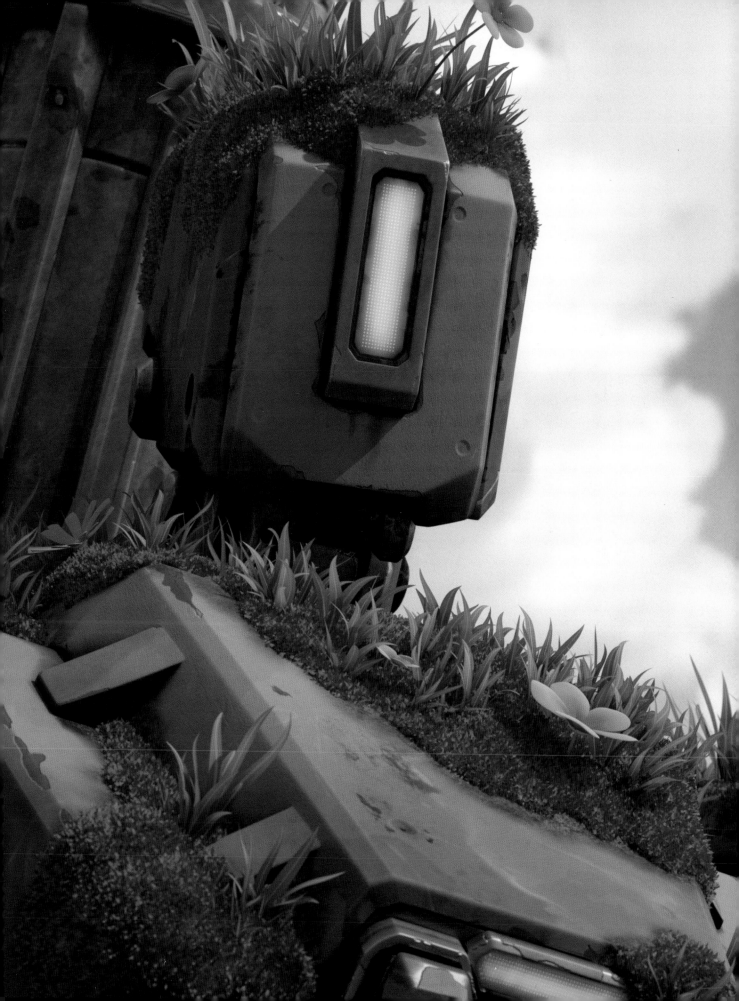

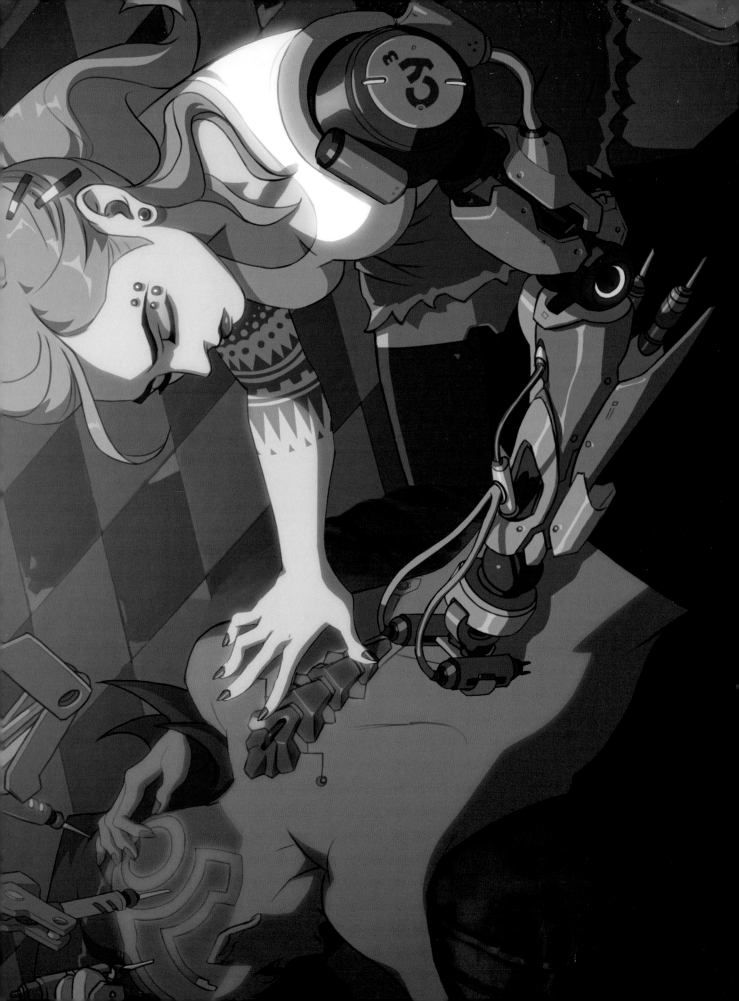

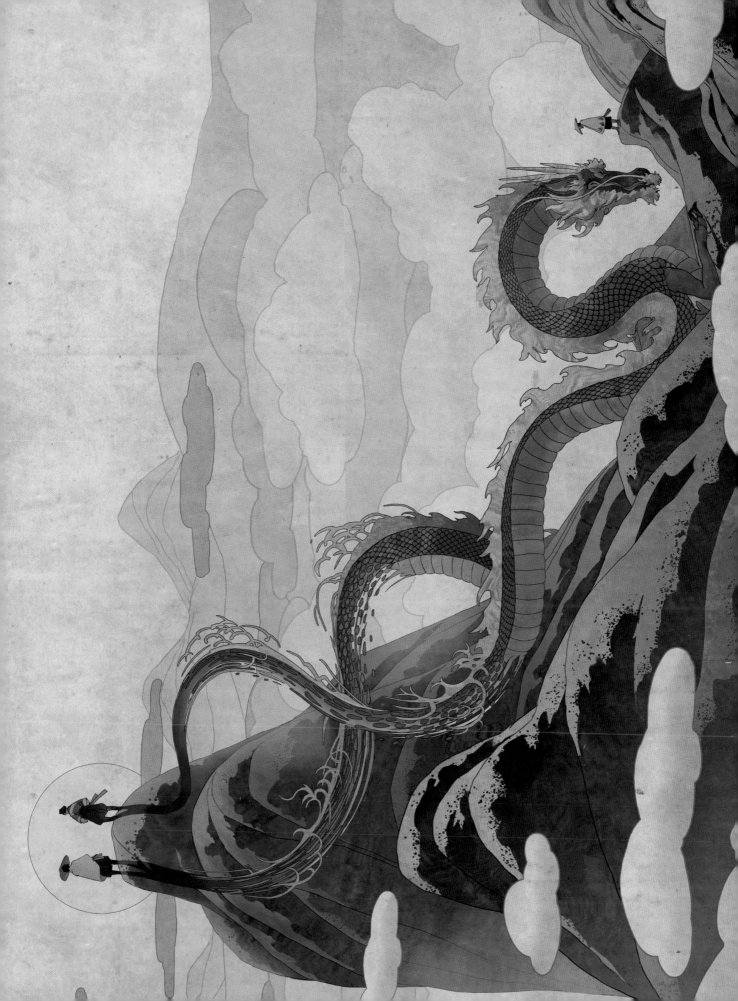

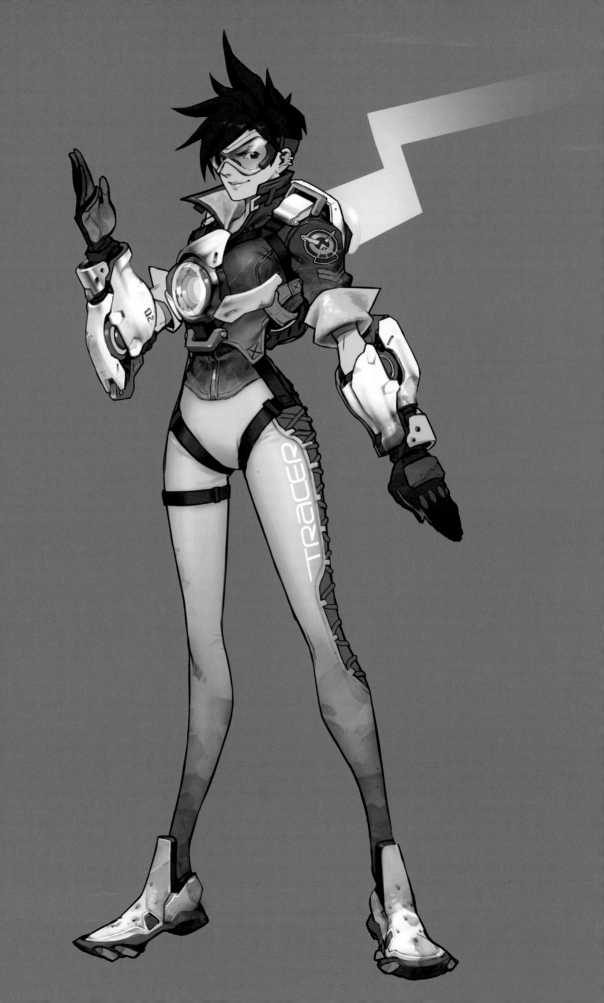

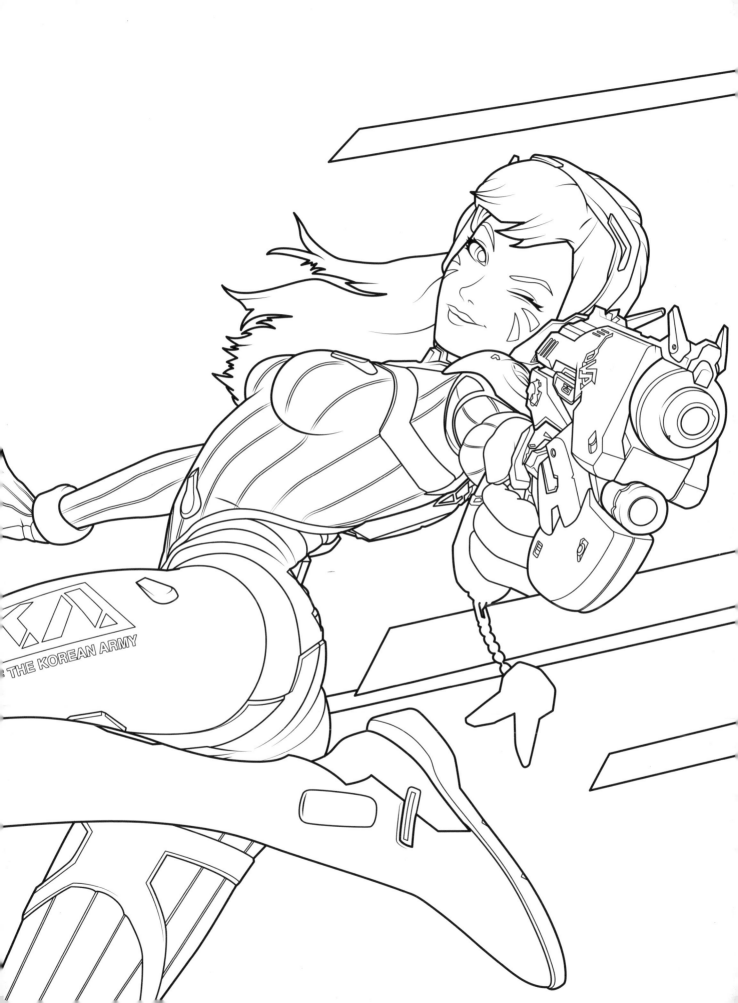

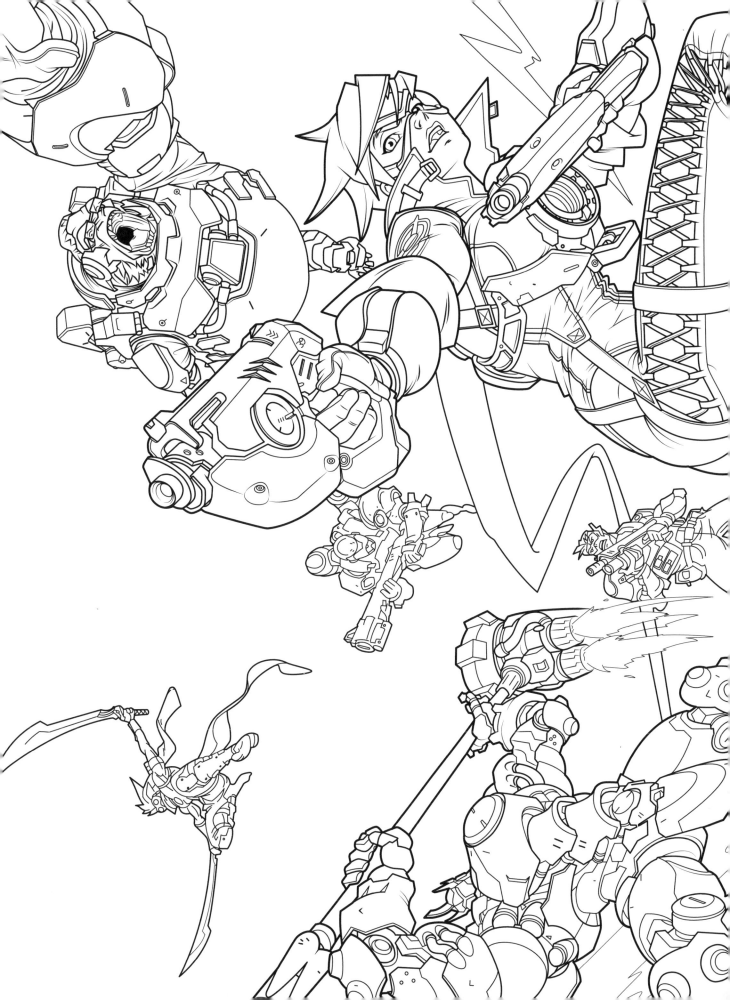

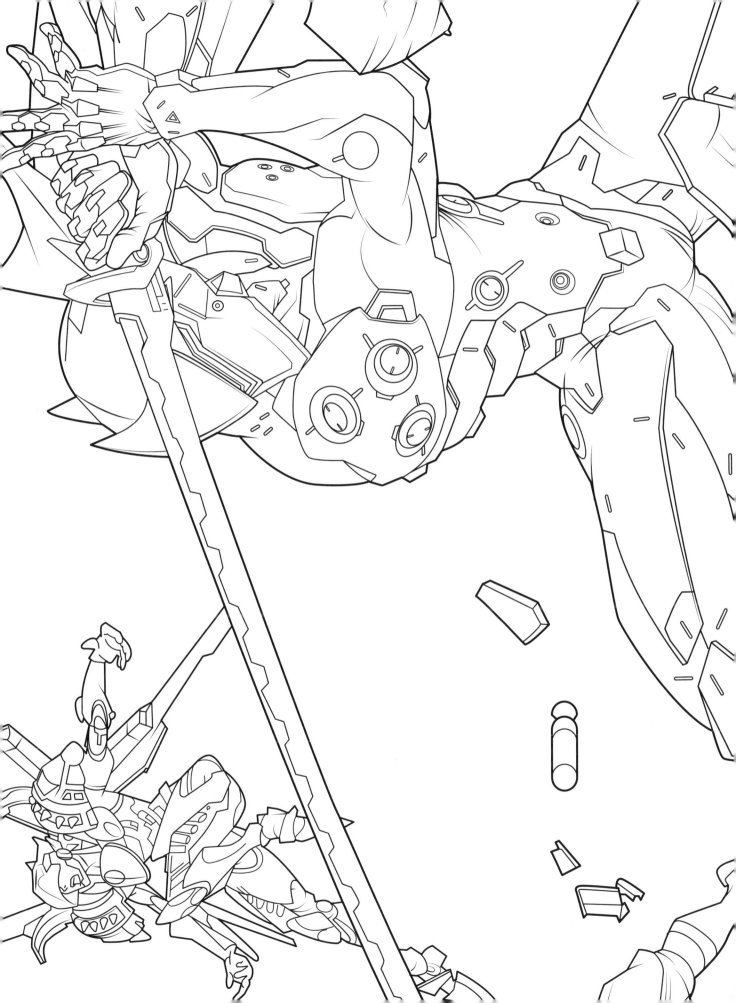

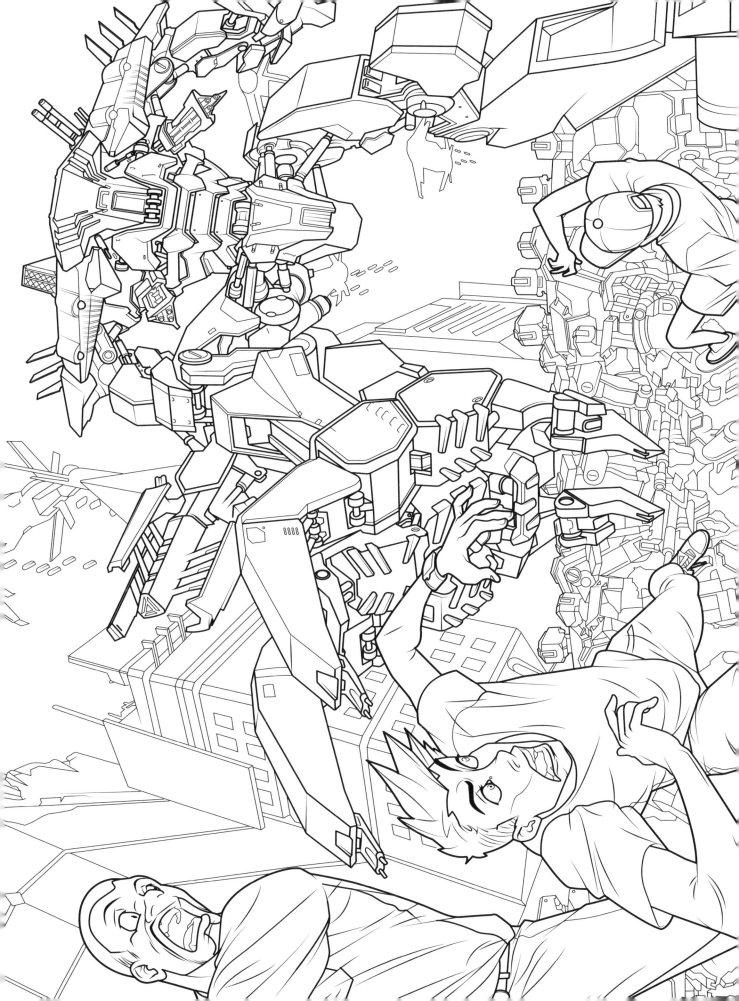

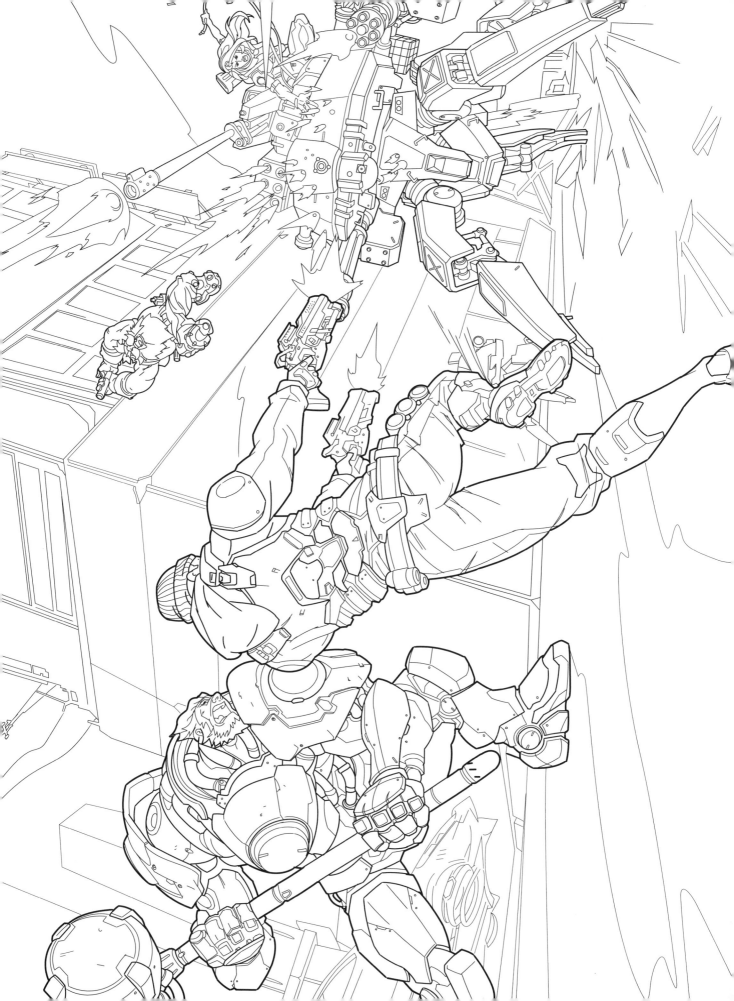

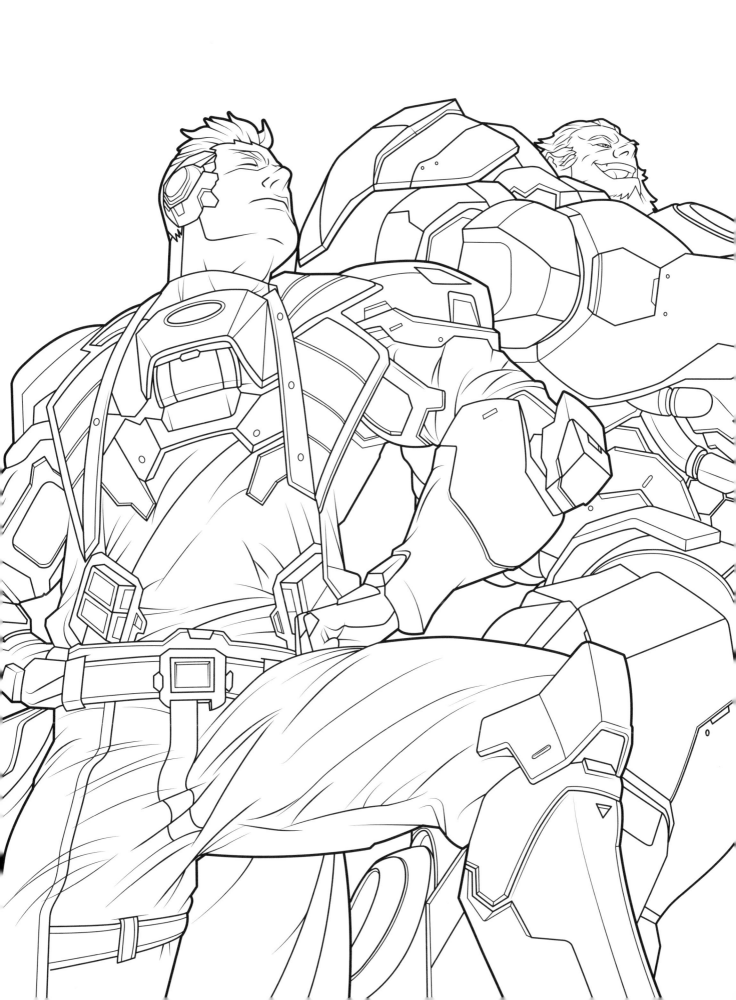

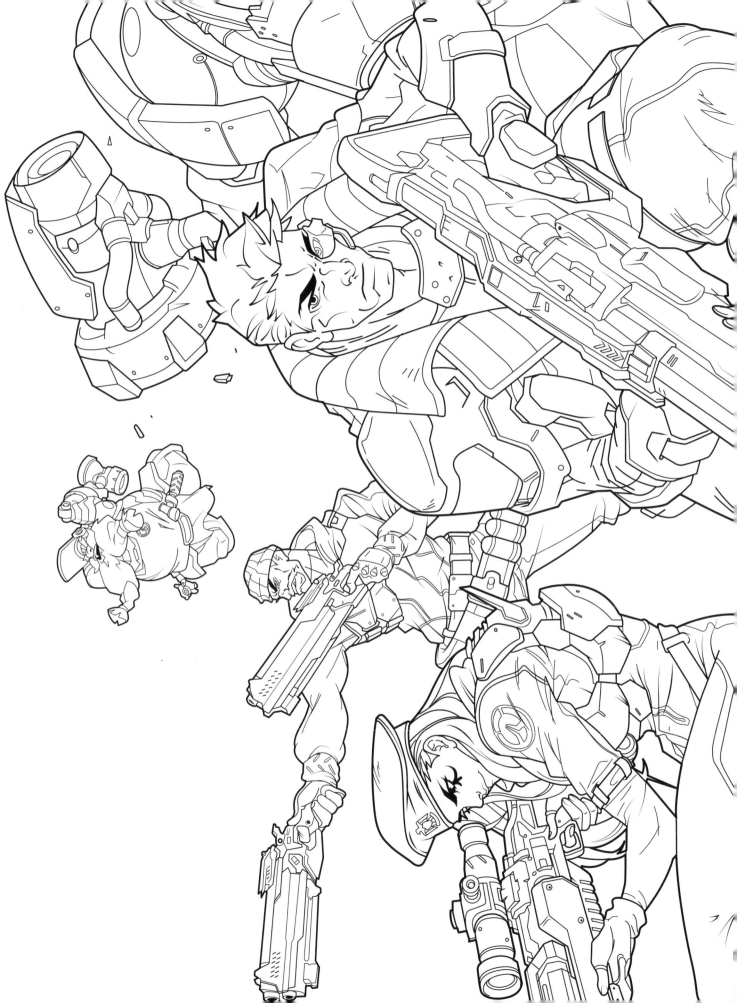

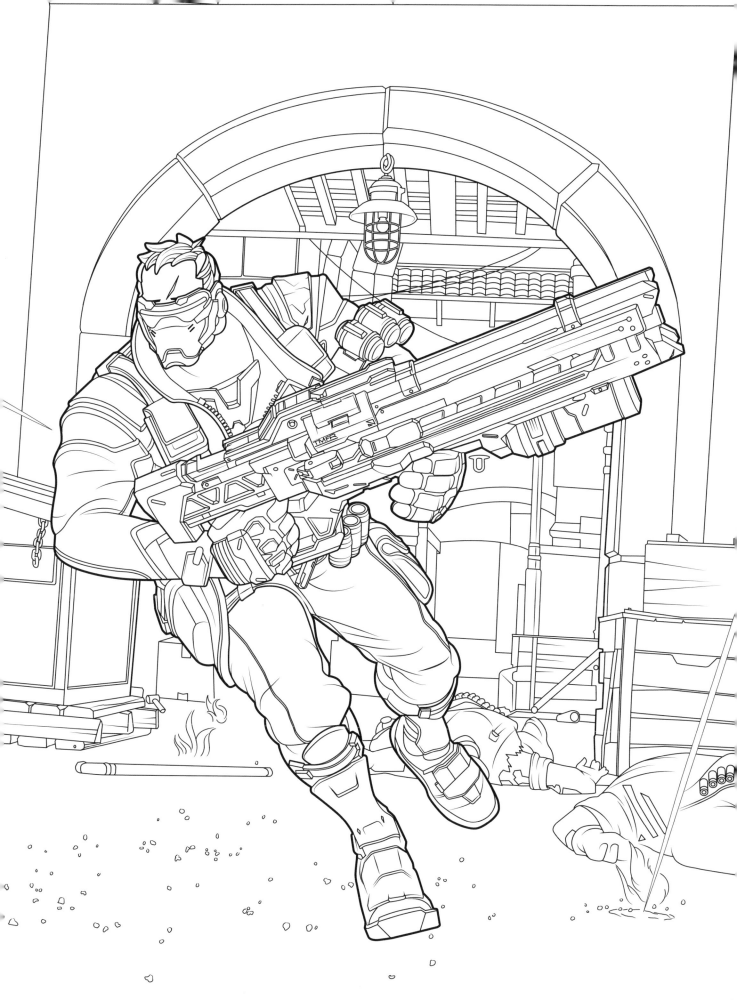

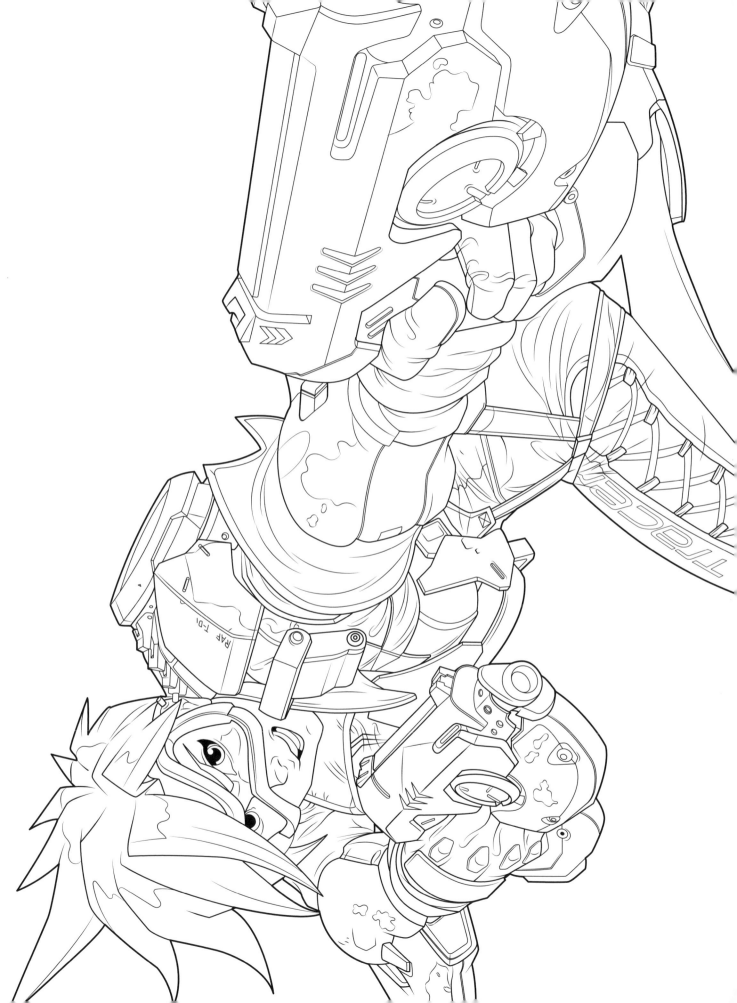

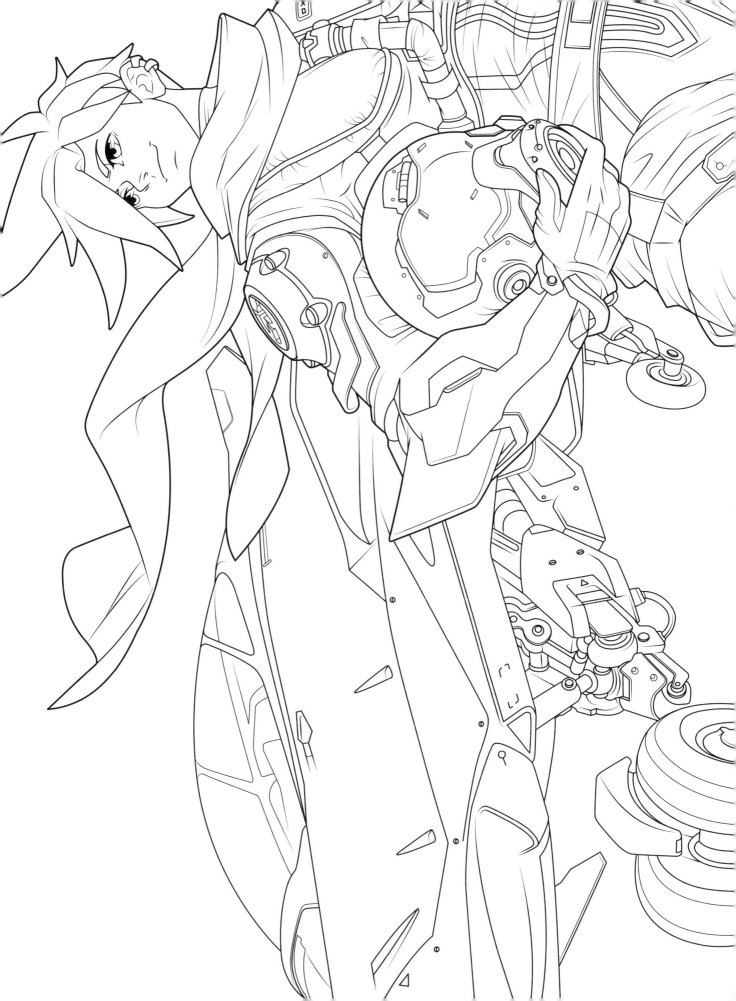

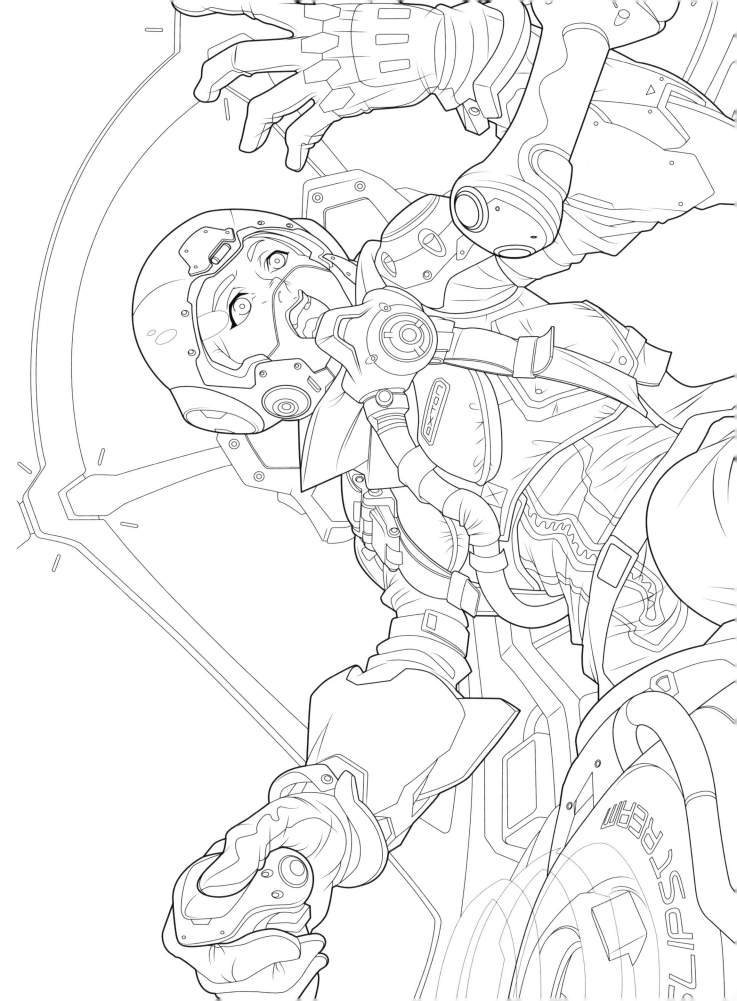

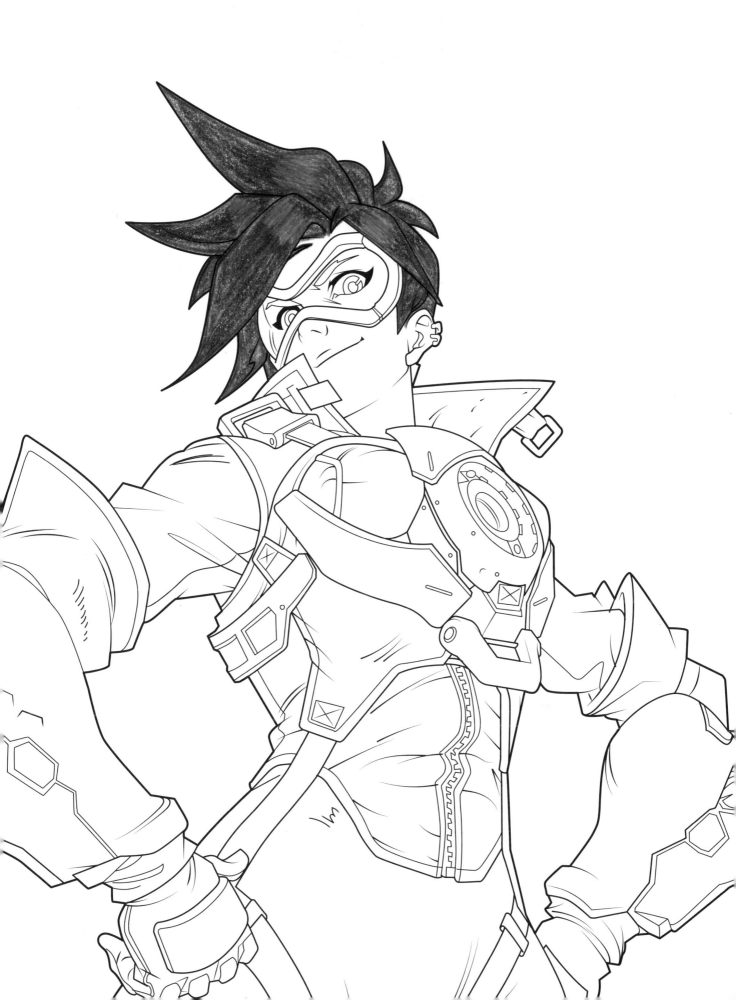

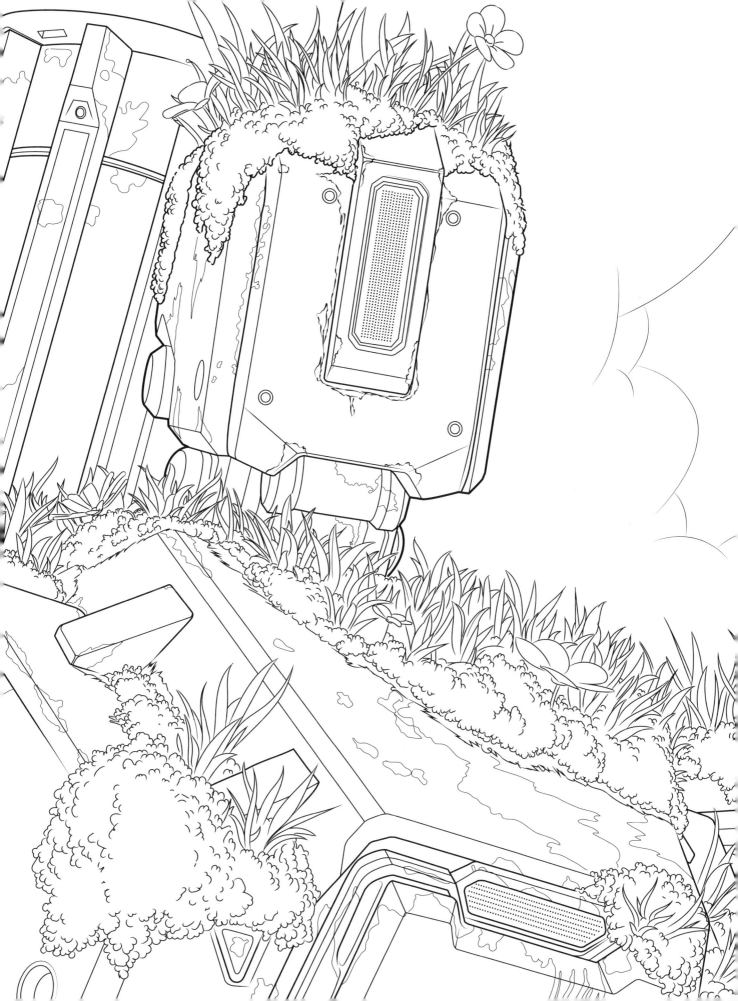

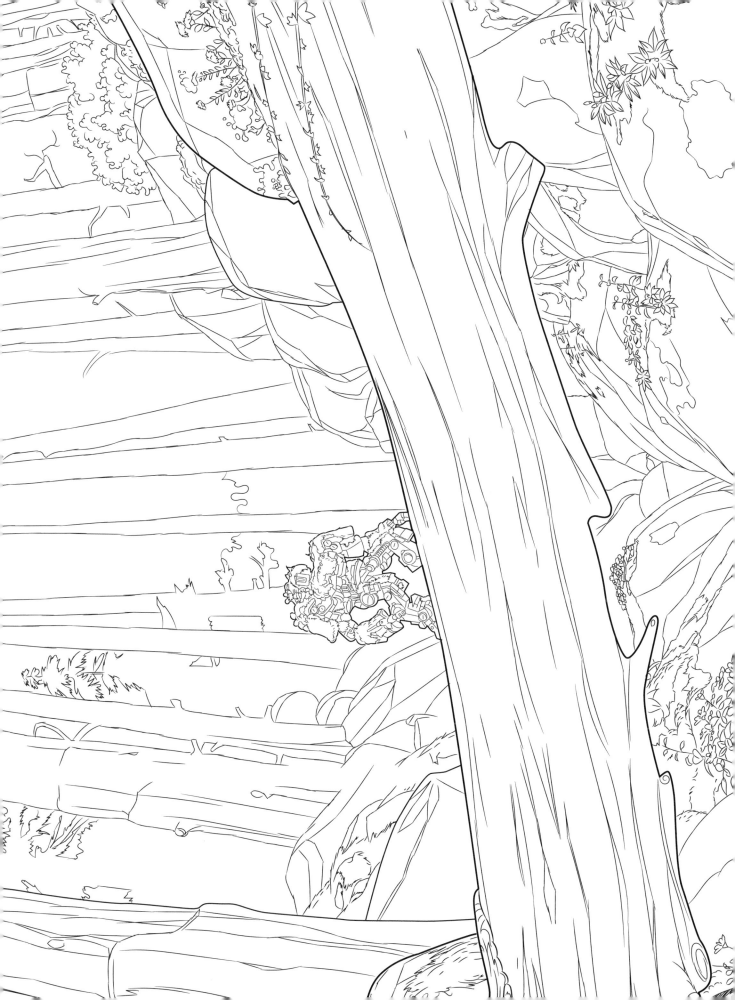

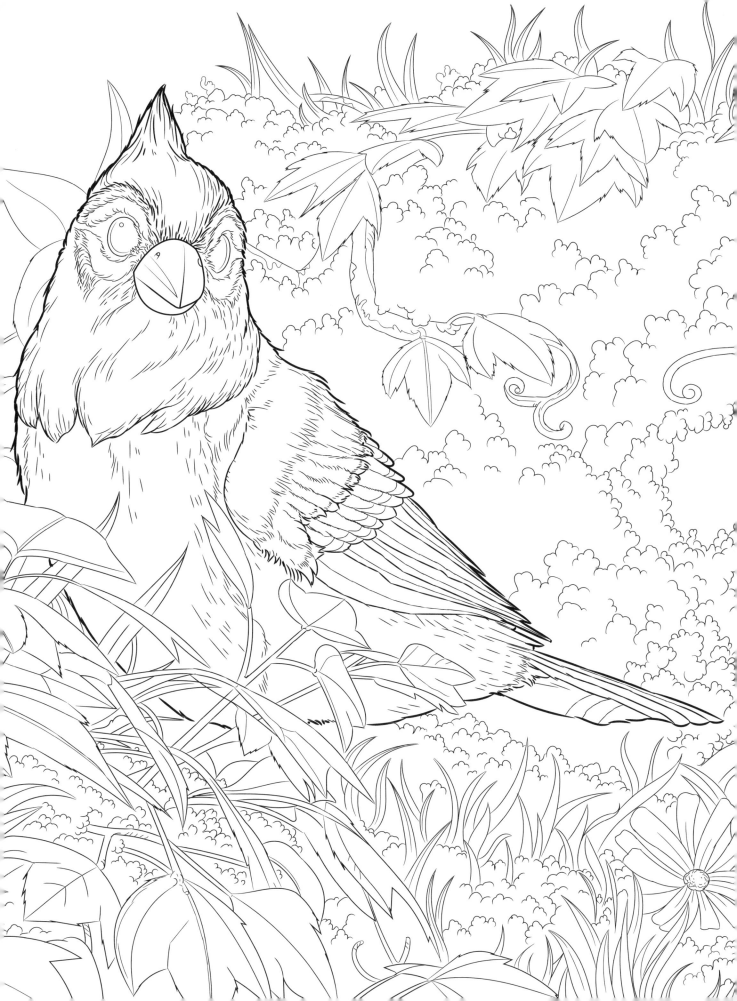

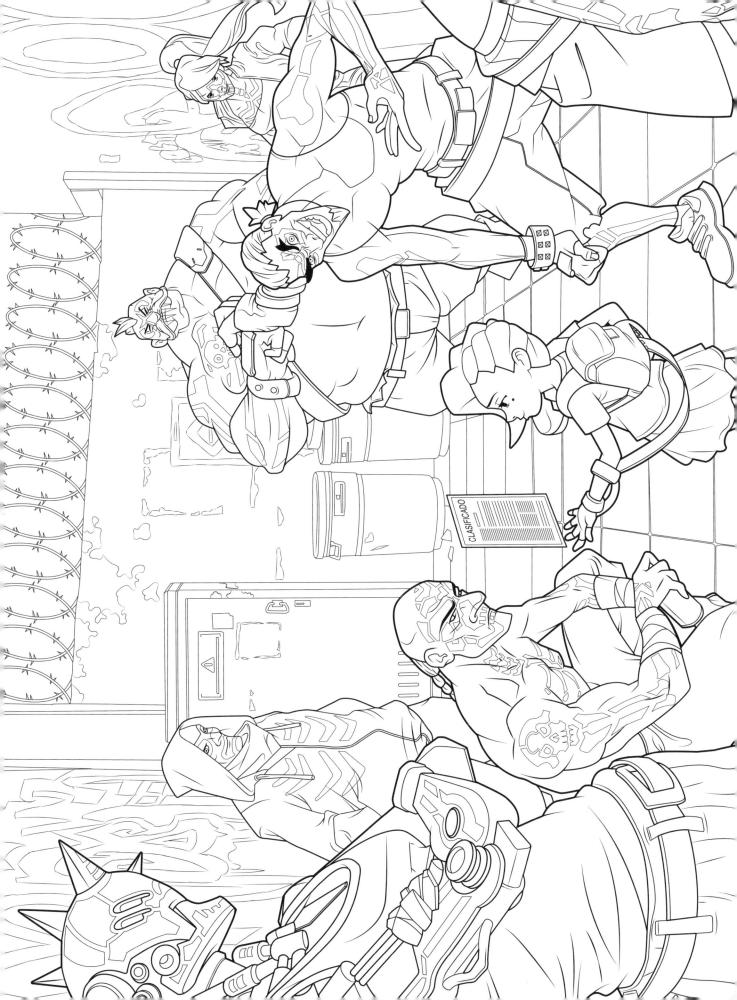

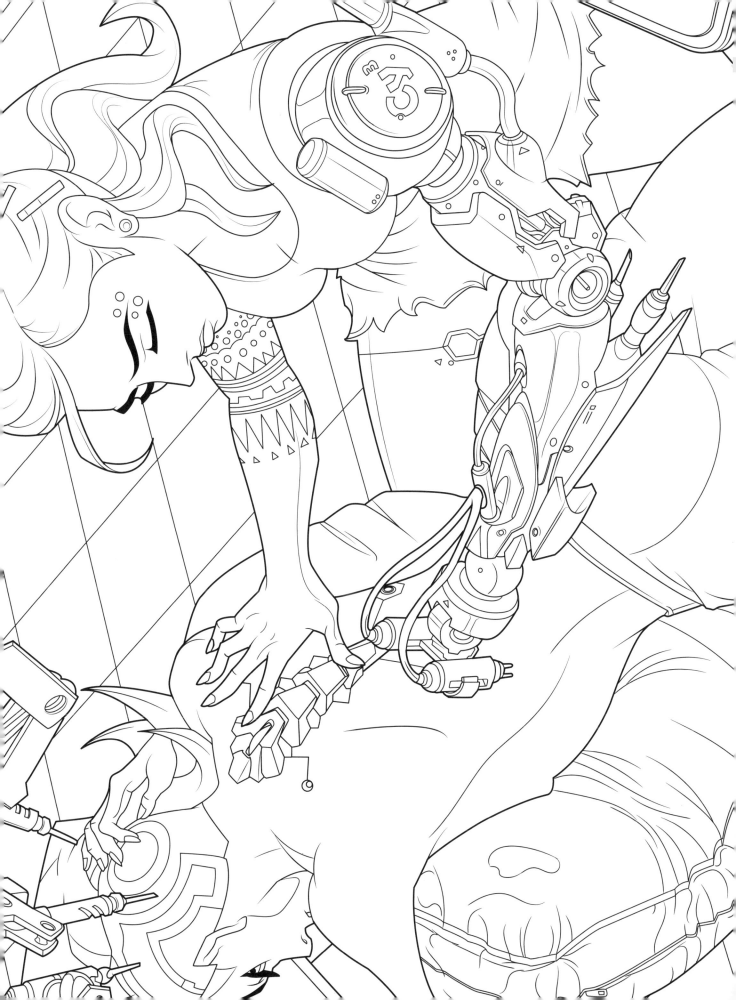

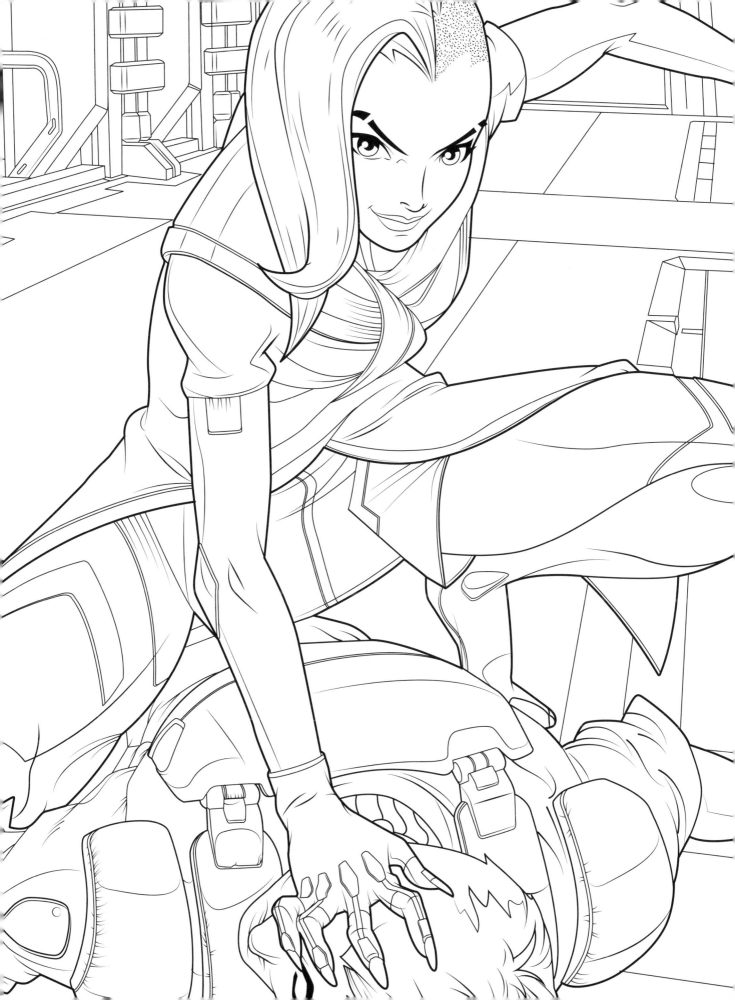

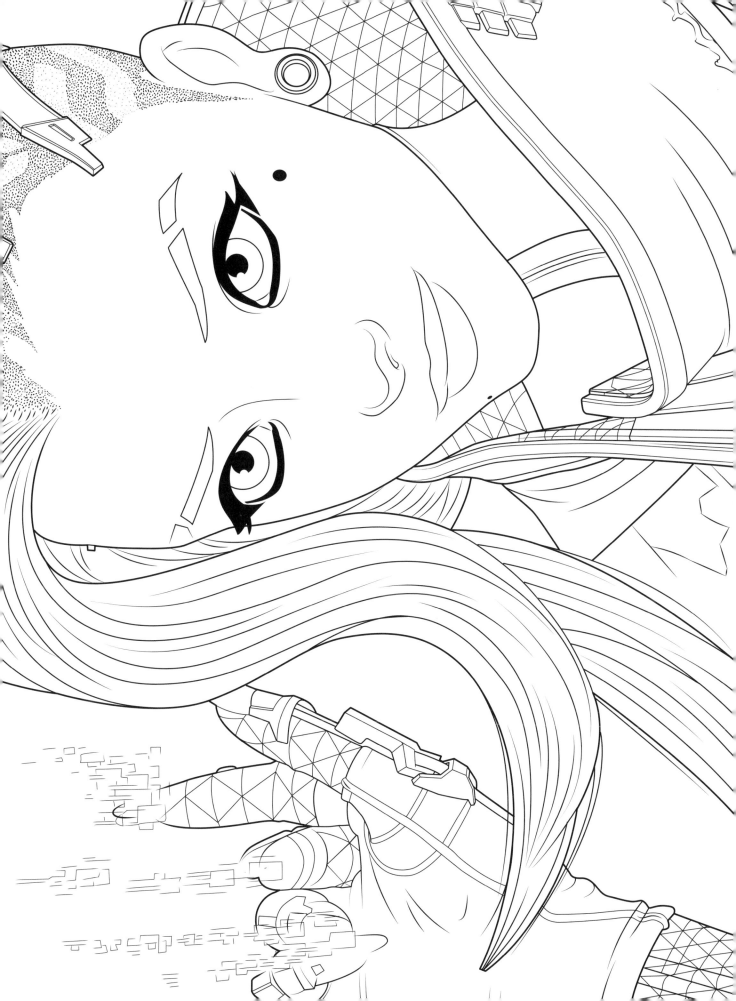

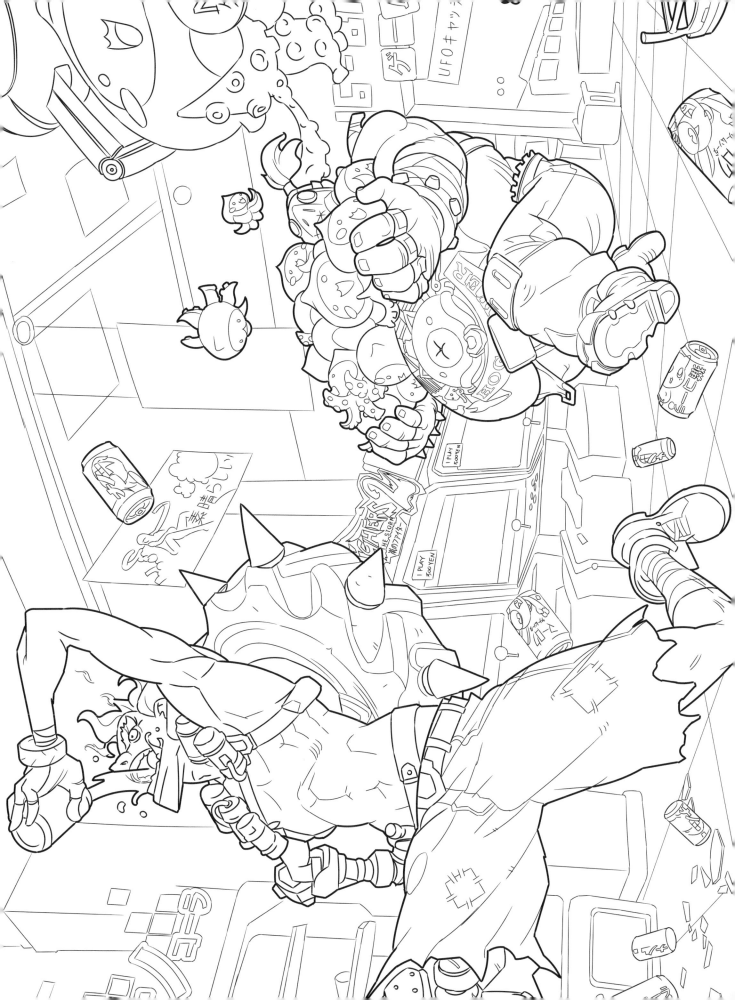

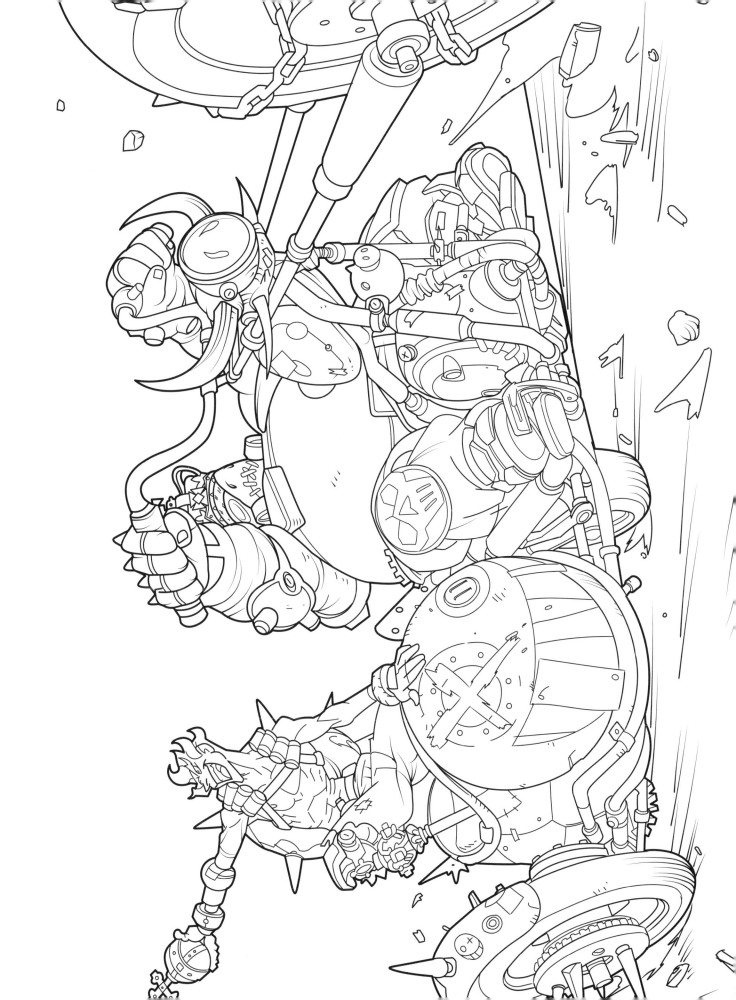

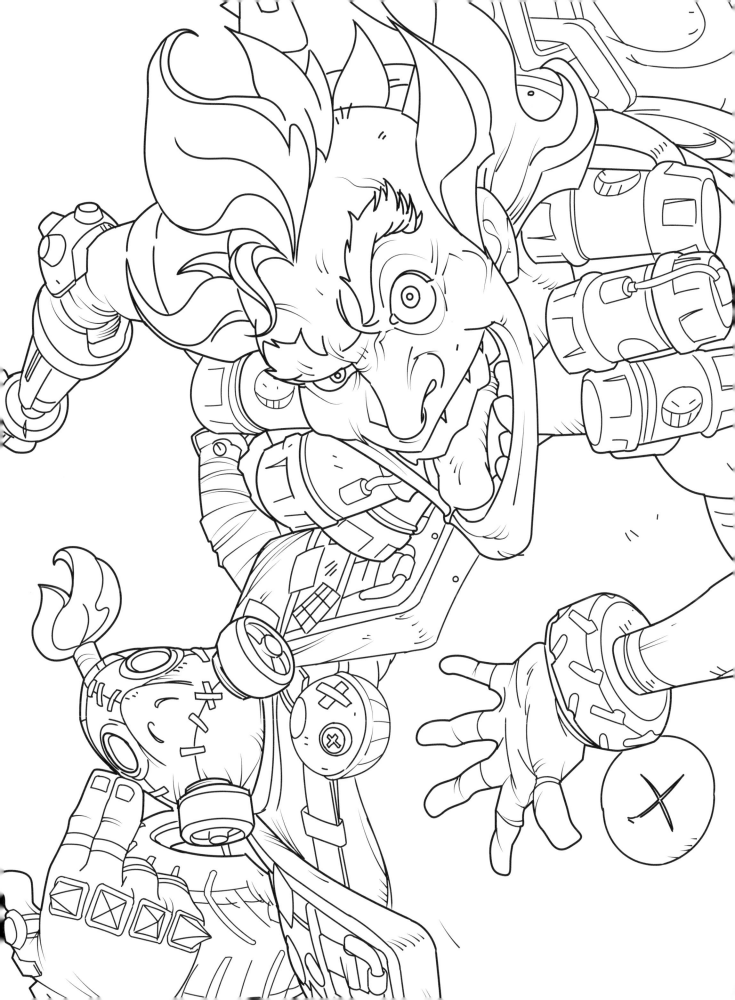

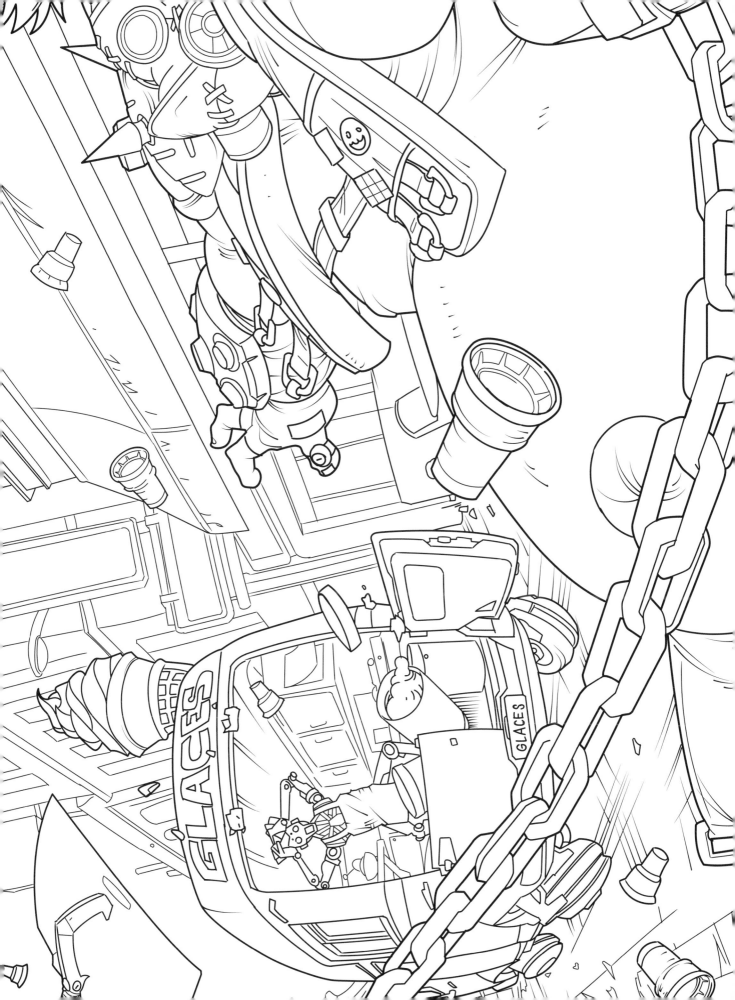

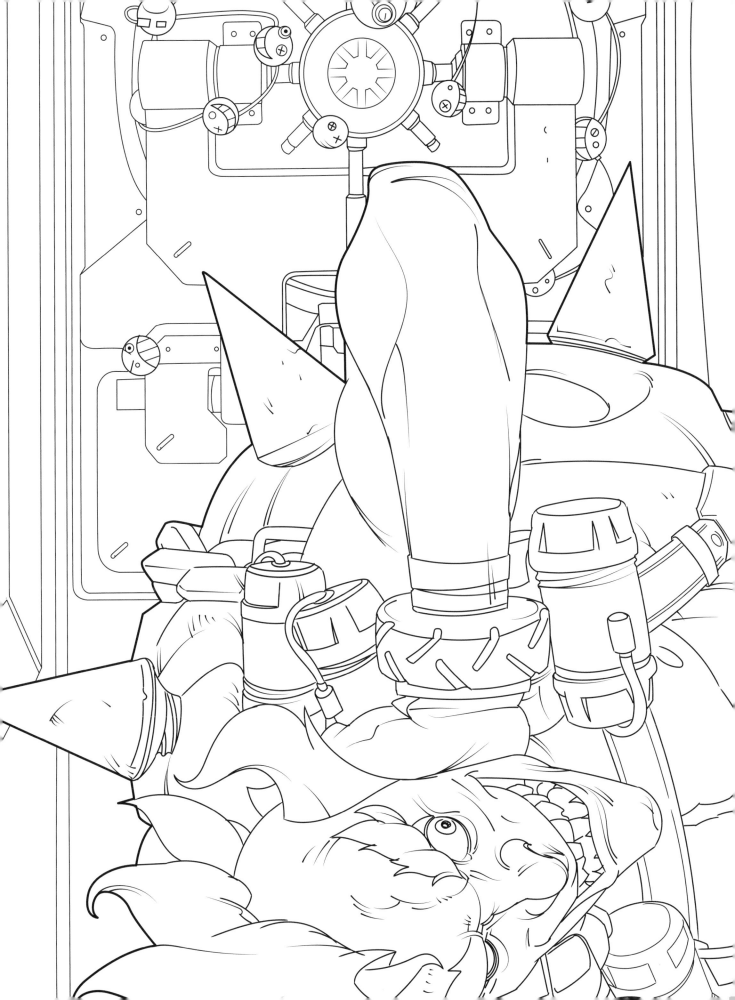

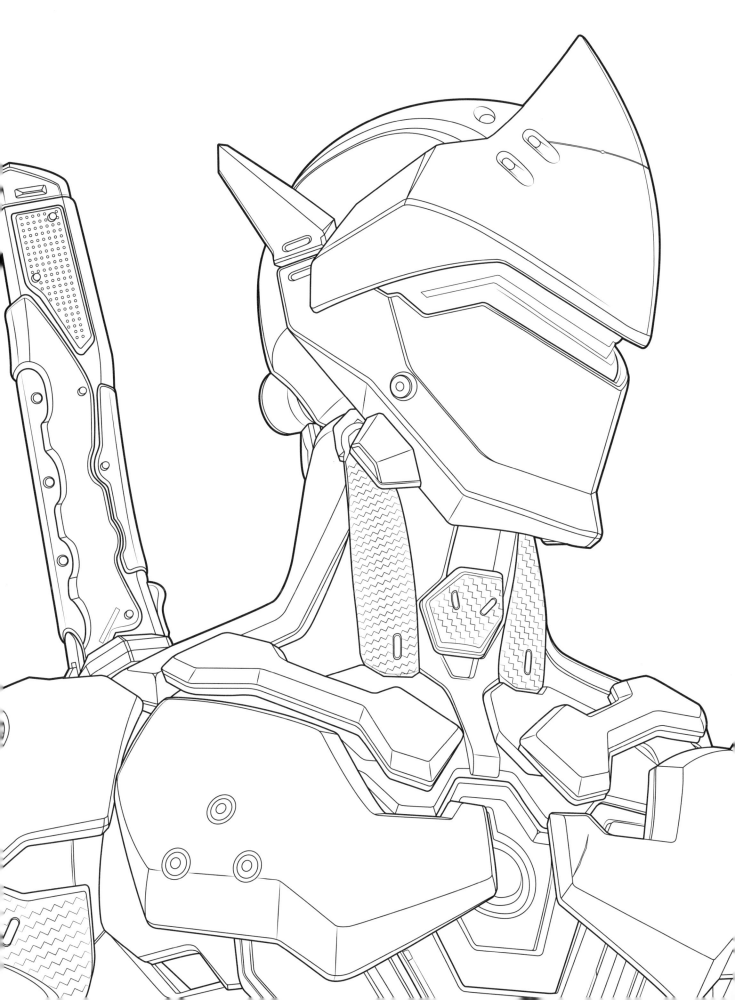

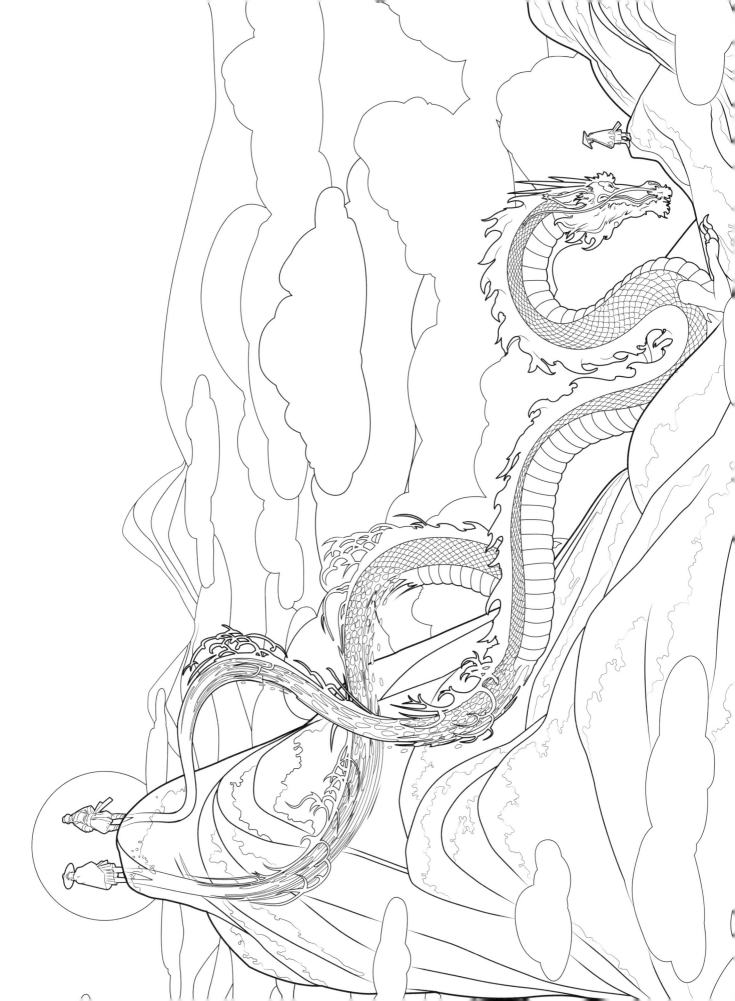

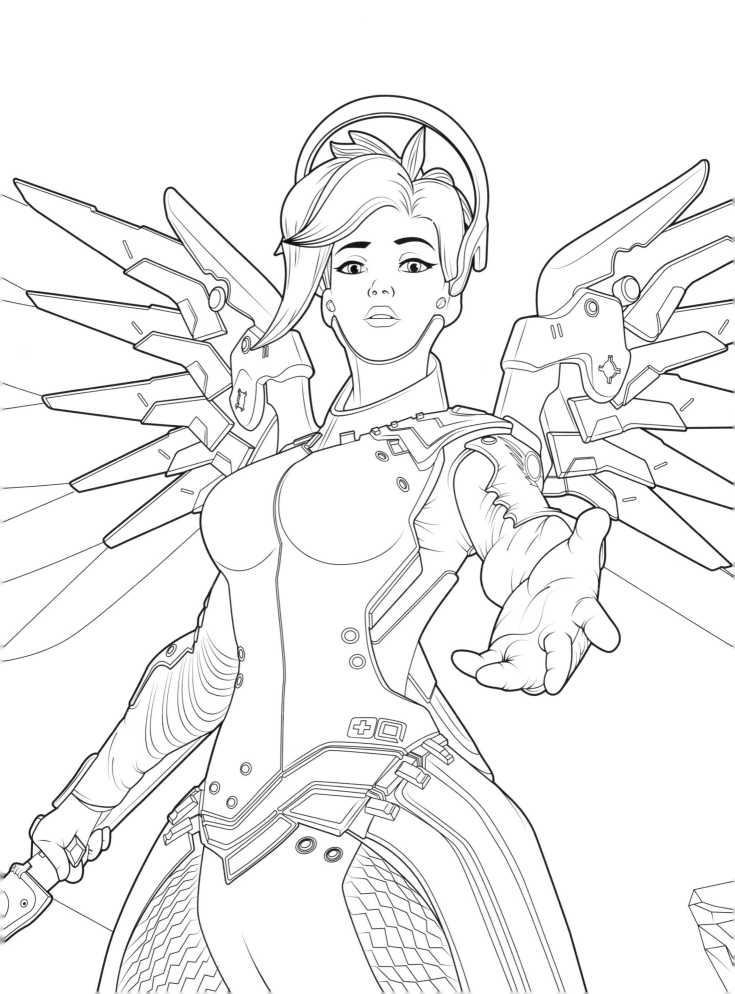

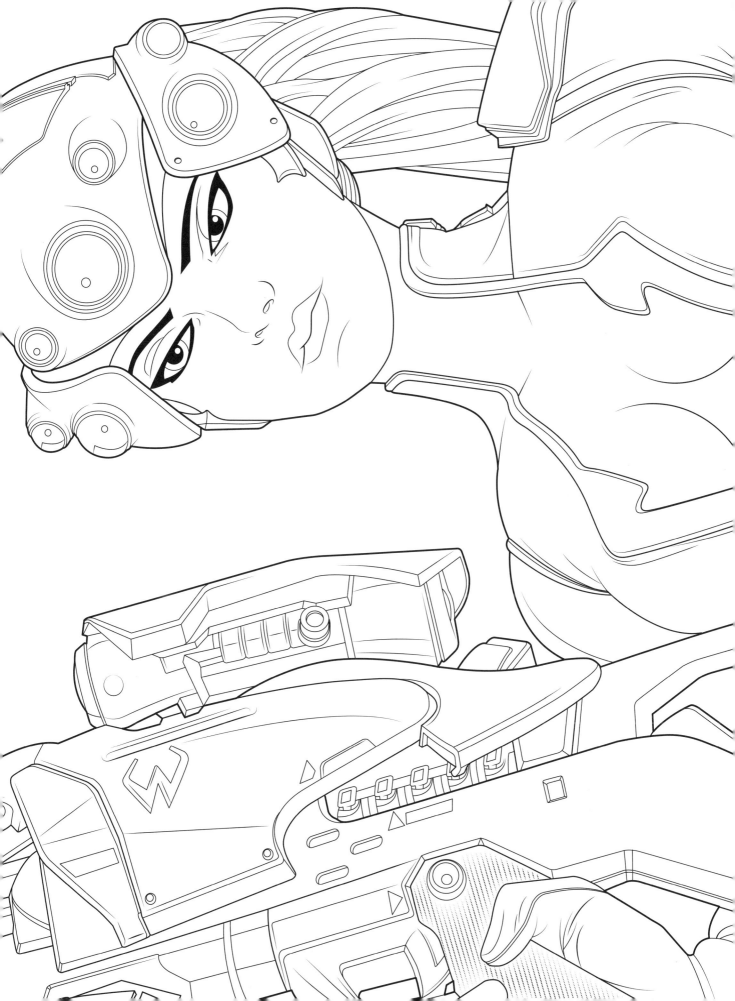

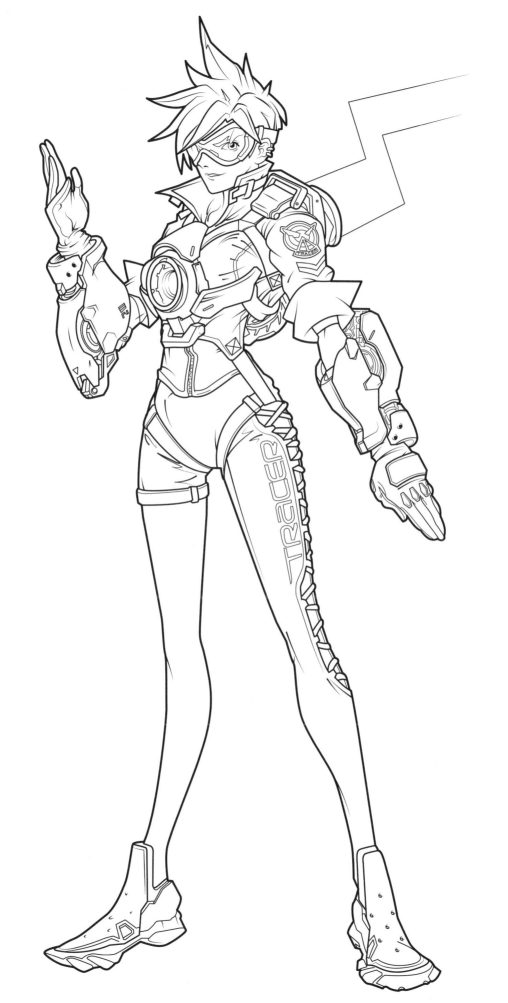

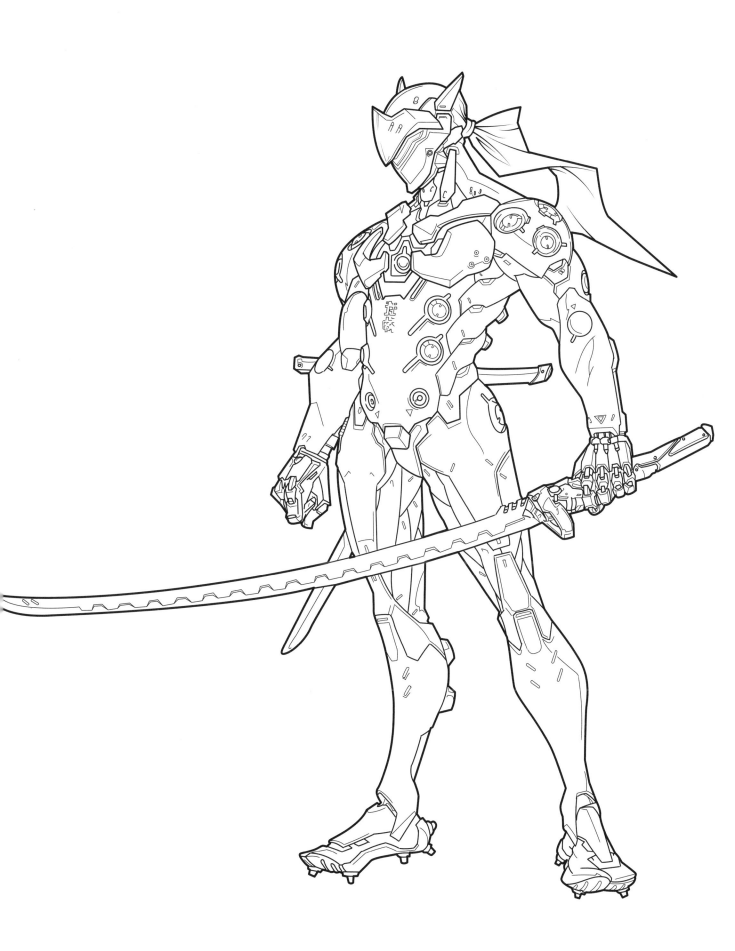

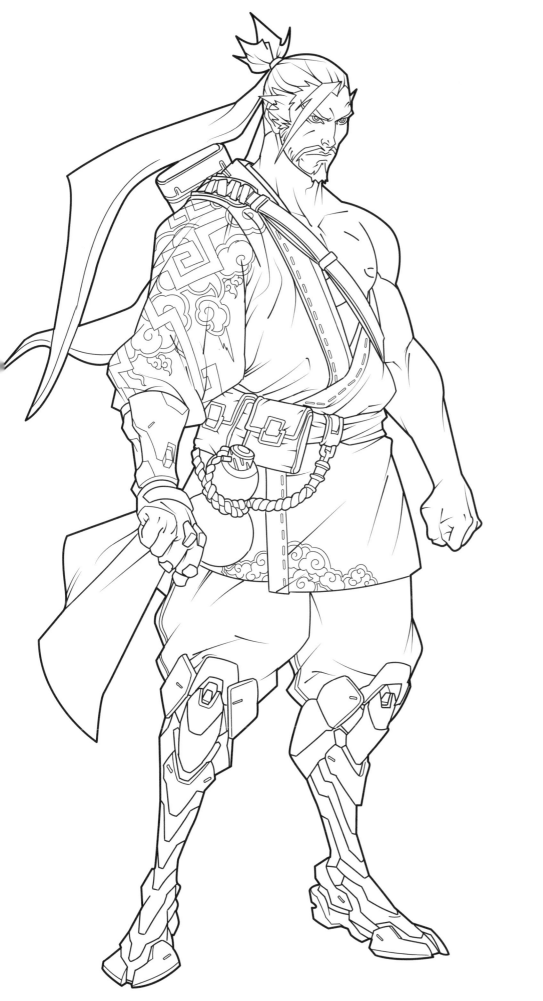

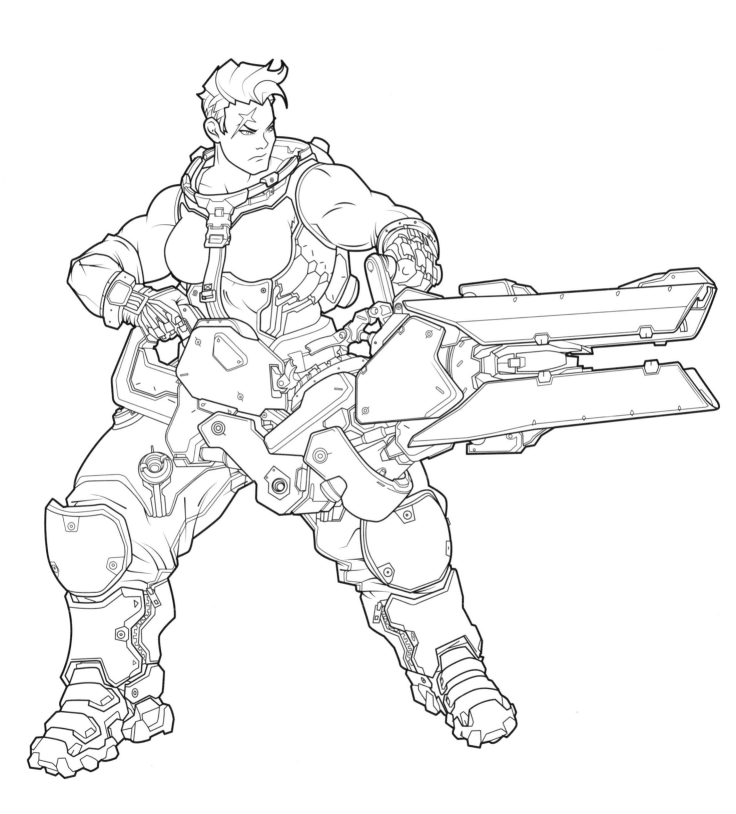

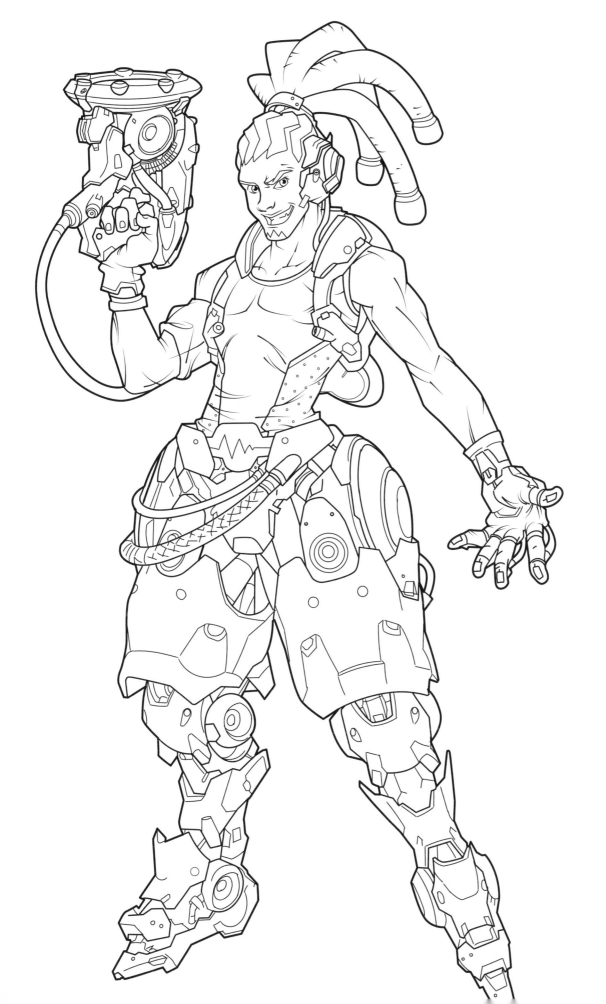

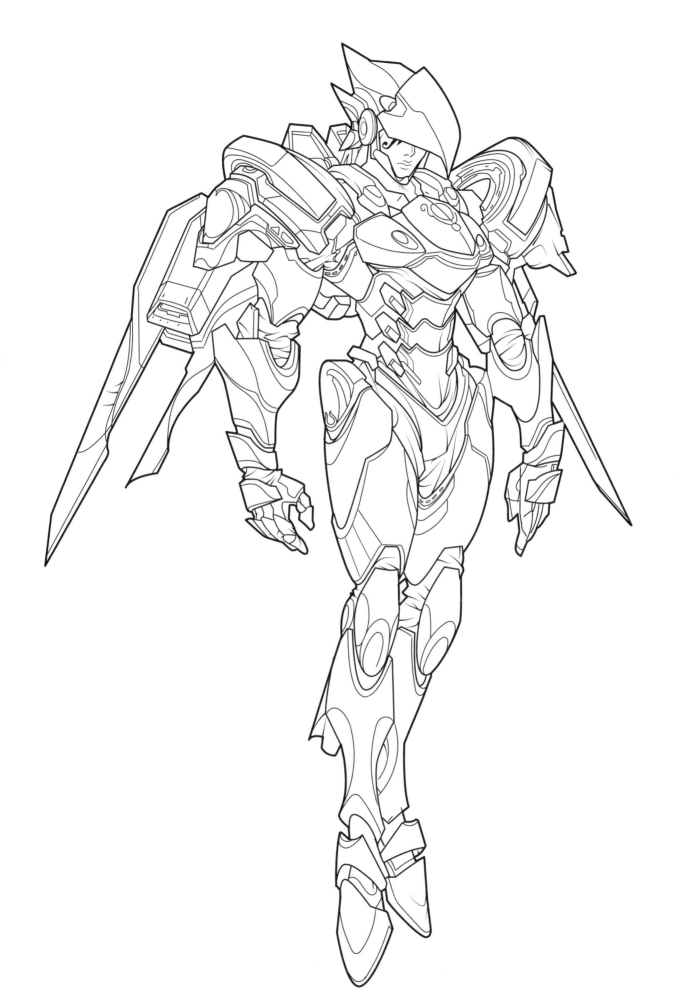

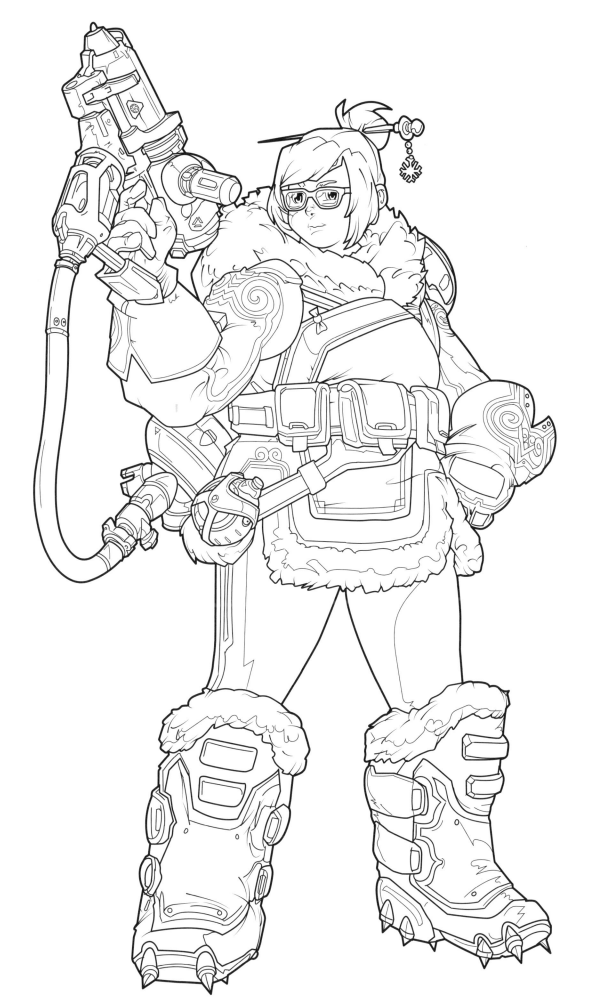

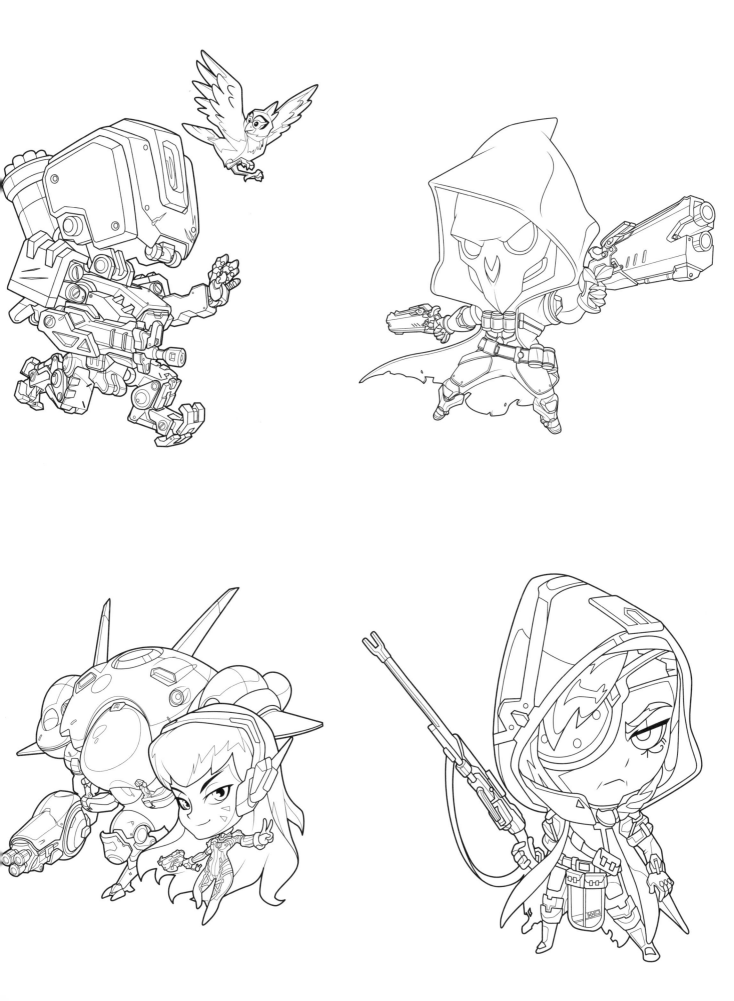

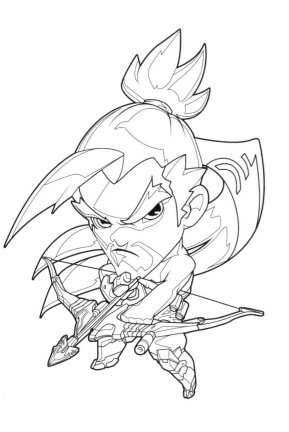
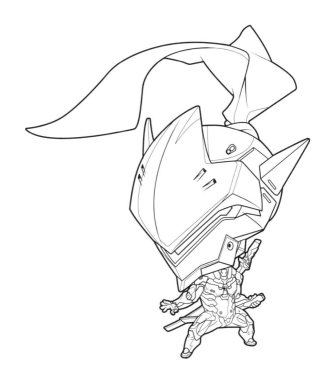
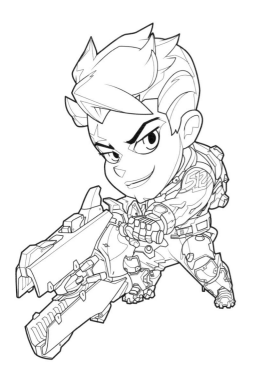
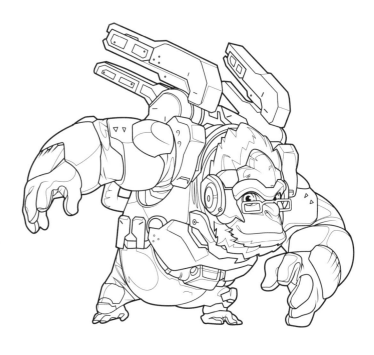

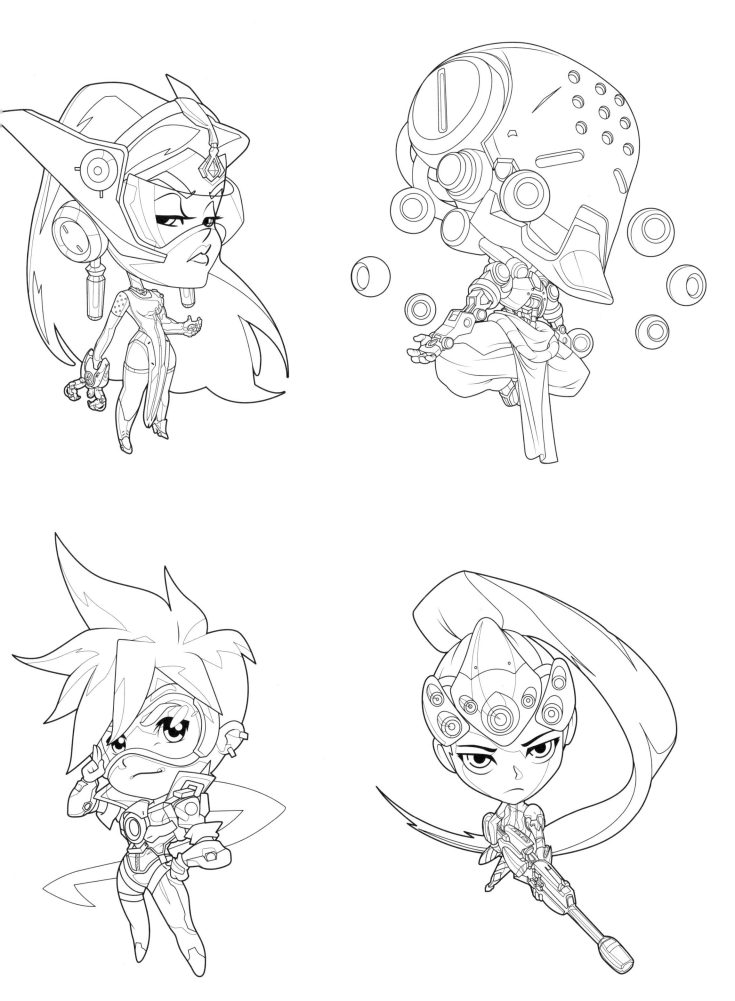

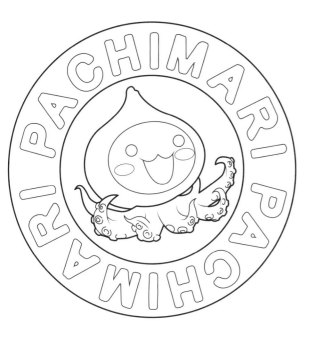

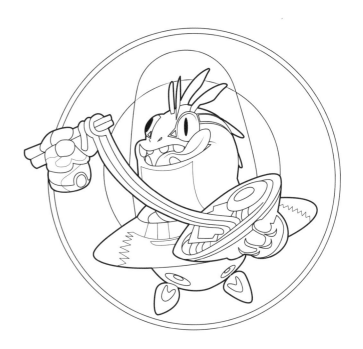

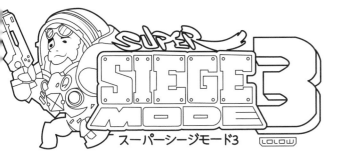

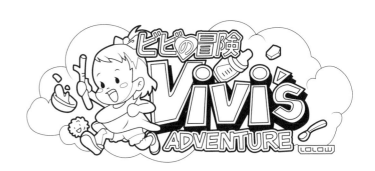

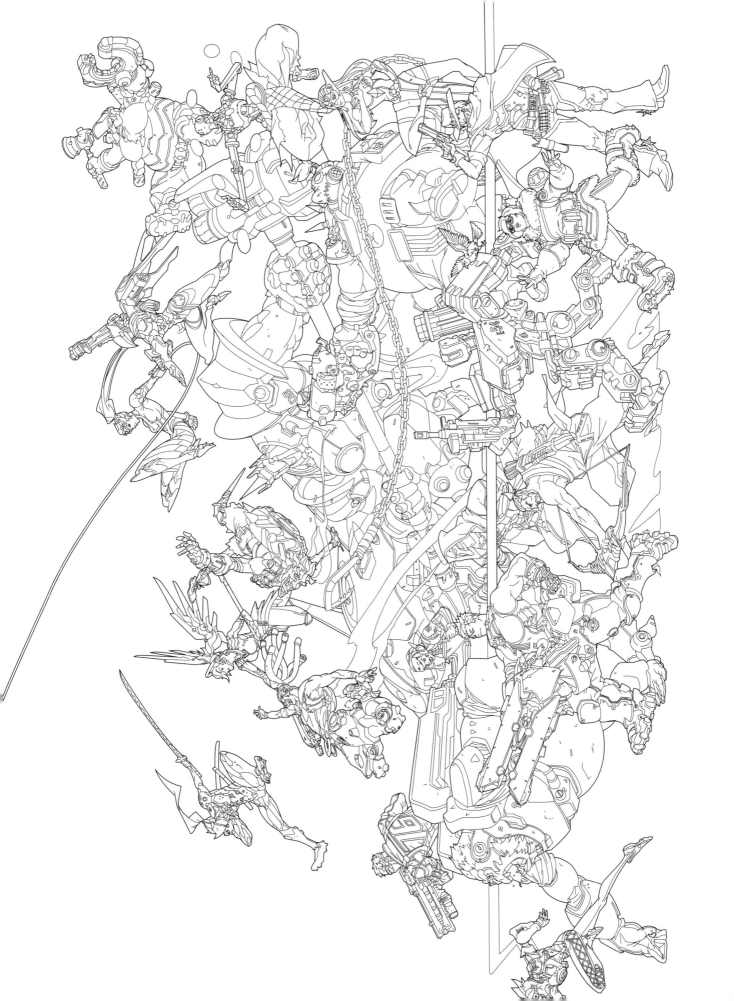